Golden Praises

Golden Praises

Compiled by Jo Petty

The C.R. Gibson Company, Norwalk, Connecticut

FOREWORD

Collected and treasured over the years, here is a volume of my favorite verses and songs of praise. Culled from many different sources, these eloquent and heartfelt praises celebrate the basic Christian virtues—mercy, love, faith, kindness, meekness—that have served as a cornerstone for all my devotional works.

These writings have been a constant source of inspiration and spiritual sustenance to me in my daily life, and I share them with you, my beloved readers, in the hope that they will set your hearts singing and spirits soaring; for we have much to sing and be joyful about as we witness God's works on earth and wait for the place He has prepared for us in His eternal kingdom.

Jo Petty

Sing
of
Mercy

Come, Thou Fount of every blessing,
Tune my heart to sing Thy grace.

ROBERT ROBINSON

Ponder anew what the Almighty can do,
If with His love He befriend me and you.

JOACHIM NEANDER

Lord, I would bless You for Your ceaseless care,
And all Your work from day to day declare!

LUCY E. G. WHITMORE

Is not my life with hourly mercies crowned?
Does not Your arm encircle me around?

LUCY E. G. WHITMORE

Your grace alone, God, to me can pardon speak.

HORATIUS BONAR

Thou of life the fountain art,
Freely let me take of Thee;
Spring thou up within my heart,
Rise to all eternity.

CHARLES WESLEY

Let Your healing voice impart the
sense of joy divine.

ANNE STEELE

I love to think on mercies past,
And future good implore,
And all my cares and sorrows cast
On Him whom I adore.

PHOEBE H. BROWNE

He stands knocking at the door of every
      sinner's heart.

CHARLES WESLEY

Listen, the Spirit is calling; Jesus
      will freely forgive.

ANNIE L. JAMES

There's mercy with the Lord!

JOHN H. STOCKTON

Tune my heart to sing Your grace;
Streams of mercy, never ceasing,
Call for songs of loudest praise.

ROBERT ROBINSON

I've found a Friend, oh, such a Friend!
So kind, and true, and tender,
So wise a Counsellor and Guide,
So mighty a defender!

JAMES G. SMALL

Great God, Your nature has no bound,
So let Your pardoning love be found.

ISAAC WATTS

When I to You lift up my eyes,
You hear my repentant sighs.

PAUL EBER

Praise Him, still the same forever, slow
to chide, and swift to bless.

HENRY F. LYTE

From every stormy wind that blows,
From every swelling tide of woes,
There is a calm, a sure retreat:
'Tis found beneath the mercy seat.

HUGH STOWELL

Praise the Lord, for He is kind.

JOHN MILTON

The heavens declare Your glory,
Lord; in every star Your wisdom shines.

ISAAC WATTS

Your tender mercies shall illume the midnight of
the soul.
Teach us, in every state, to make Your will our
own.

AUGUSTUS M. TOPLADY

Jesus comes again in mercy when our hearts
are bowed with care.

GODFREY THRING

I praise You for Your mercies past and humbly
hope for more.

JOSEPH ADDISON

There's mercy with the Lord, and He will surely
give you rest.

JOHN H. STOCKTON

When sickness fills my heart with fear, tis sweet
to know that You are near.

JAMES EDMESTON

Earth has no sorrows that heaven cannot heal.

THOMAS MOORE

The way may be weary, and thorny the road,
but how can I falter? My help is in God.

ANONYMOUS

New mercies, each returning day,
Hover around us while we pray.

JOHN KEBLE

His mercies shall endure.
Ever faithful, ever sure.

JOHN MILTON

Thy mercies how tender! How firm to the end!
Our Maker, Defender, Redeemer and Friend.

ROBERT GRANT

Jesus comes again in answer, to an earnest
     heart-felt prayer.

GODFREY THRING.

His mercy waneth never: God is wisdom, God
     is love.

JOHN BOWRING

Make the fruits of grace abound; bring
     relief for all complaints.

JOHN NEWTON

Green pastures are before me.

ANNA L. WARING

God's grace will to the end stronger and
     brighter shine.

ANNE STEELE

When all Your mercies, O my God,
My rising soul surveys,
Transported with the view, I'm lost
In wonder, love, and praise.

JOSEPH ADDISON

The opening year Your mercy shows.

PHILIP DODDRIDGE

He clothes me with His love; upholds me with
    His truth.

JAMES MONTGOMERY

Sing of Love

God is love:
His mercy brightens all the paths we rove.
JOHN BOWRING

I open wide my heart to You; here, Lord, abide!
GEORG WEISSEL

As far from danger as from fear,
While Love, almighty Love, is near.
CHARLES WESLEY

Sing praise to God who reigns above,
the God of all creation,
the God of power,
the God of love.

JOHANN J. SCHUTZ

Your glory flames from sun and star.
OLIVER WENDELL HOLMES

As the branch is in the vine,
I am His and He is mine.

WILLIAM McCOMB

Christ is our Guide and Friend;
His love shall never end!

CHRISTIAN H. BATEMAN

Lord, where harvests ripen, You are there.

CHRISTOPHER WORDSWORTH

For all Your love, we bless You.

SARAH DOUDNEY

How wise Your bounteous love is spread!

SAMUEL LONGFELLOW

Grace, like the Lord, never fails from
    age to age.

JOHN NEWTON

I'll consecrate my life to You, my Savior
    and my God!

RALPH E. HUDSON

Whosoever will, whosoever will,
Send the proclamation over vale and hill;
'Tis a loving Father calls the wanderer home,
Whosoever will may come.

PHILIP P. BLISS

Redeemer, Savior, Friend, You have died for all.

WILLIAM H. CLARK

By You life's path is brightened with
    sunshine and with song.

SARAH DOUDNEY

What am I that He should show so much love
    to me?

ANONYMOUS

Dear Savior, let me call You mine;
    I cannot wish for more.

ANNE STEELE

He rules the world with truth and grace,
And makes the nations prove
The glories of His righteousness,
And wonders of His love.

ISAAC WATTS

All praise and glory be to Thee
For wisdom, power and majesty.

JOHAN OLOF WALLIN

We'll crowd Your gates with thankful songs.

ISAAC WATTS

Love that found me, wondrous thought!
Found me when I sought Him not.

WILLIAM McCOMB

Teach me, in every state, to make Your will
    my own.

AUGUSTUS M. TOPLADY

Here, Lord, I give myself away.

ISAAC WATTS

New every morning is Your love.

JOHN KEBLE

O that the world might taste and
see the riches of His grace!

CHARLES WESLEY

All to You, our God, we owe,
Source whence all our blessings flow.

ANNA L. BARBAULD

I love my tender Shepherd's voice;
I love the peaceful fold.

HORATIUS BONAR

God is with me—God, my everlasting light.

THOMAS KELLY

Oh what a wonder that Jesus loves me!

PHILIP P. BLISS

Let us love our Lord supremely; let us love
each other, too.

GEORGE ATKINS

Praise to God, immortal praise,
For the love that crowns our days.

ANNA L. BARBAULD

Teach me Thy steps to trace,
learning how to love from Thee.

JANE E. LEESON

O love, how gracious is Thy way!

JOHN WESLEY

How shall we show our love to You, Lord, who
gives all?

CHRISTOPHER WORDSWORTH

Savior, teach me day by day,
Love's sweet lesson to obey.

JANE E. LEESON

O may my love to Thee
Pure, warm, and changeless be.

RAY PALMER

What shall I do my God to love, my loving
God to praise!

CHARLES WESLEY

In a love which cannot cease, I am His, and
He is mine.

GEORGE W. ROBINSON

God is our strength and song, and His
    salvation ours.

JAMES MONTGOMERY

O dearly, dearly has He loved, and I must
    love Him, too.

CECIL F. ALEXANDER

Proclaim to every people, tongue,
and nation that God, in whom they live
and move, is Love.

MARY A. THOMSON

My hope I cannot measure,
The path to life is free;
My Savior has my treasure,
And He will walk with me.

ANNA L. WARING

The King of love my Shepherd is,
I nothing lack if I am His,
And He is mine forever.

HENRY W. BAKER

To worship rightly is to love each other.

JOHN GREENLEAF WHITTIER

How sweet, how heavenly is the sight,
When those who love the Lord
In one another's peace delight,
And so fulfill His Word!

JOSEPH SWAIN

Fill your barns with store,
To your God and to your brother
Give more.

THEODORE C. WILLIAMS

Help us to help each other, Lord, each
            other's cross to bear.

CHARLES WESLEY

Blest be the tie that binds
Our hearts in Christian love;
The fellowship of kindred minds
Is like to that above.

JOHN FAWCETT

O for grace our hearts to soften!
Teach us, Lord, at length to love;
We, alas! forget too often
What a Friend we have above.

JOHN NEWTON

All coldness far from my heart remove;
    may my every act, word, thought, be love.

JOHN WESLEY

Tell it to Jesus, tell it to Jesus,
He is a friend that's well-known;
You've no other such a friend or brother,
Tell it to Jesus alone.

JEREMIAH E. RANKIN

There shall be showers of blessing:
This is the promise of love.
There shall be seasons refreshing,
Sent from the Savior above.

DANIEL W. WHITTLE

God has been merciful to me!

CORNELIUS ELVEN

In Your love forever living, I must be
    forever blessed.

RAY PALMER

Father, in whom we live,
In whom we are, and move,
The glory, power, and praise receive
For Thy creating love.

CHARLES WESLEY

God, in the Gospel of His Son
Makes His eternal counsels known;
Where love in all its glory shines,
And truth is drawn in fairest lines.

BENJAMIN BEDDOME

Jesus reigns, and heaven rejoices;
Jesus reigns, the God of love.

THOMAS KELLY

With my voice to Thee uplifted,
I would praise Thy wondrous love,
May my thankful heart be gifted
With sweet music from above.

LUDAEMILIA ELIZABETH OF SCHWARZBURG-RUDOLSTADT

Lord, let me never, never outlive my love to Thee.

BERNARD OF CLAIRVAUX

Sing of Joy

Come, we that love the Lord,
And let our joys be known;
Join in a song with sweet accord,
And thus surround the throne.

ISAAC WATTS

Listen to the wondrous story
Which we chant in hymns of joy:
Glory in the highest, glory!
Glory be to God most high!

JOHN CAWOOD

He whose hope on God is founded
Has a wealth of joy unbounded.

ANONYMOUS

His Kingdom cannot fail; worship and thanks to
    Him belong.

ROBERT A. WEST

O the precious Name of Jesus!
    How it thrills my soul with joy.

LYDIA BAXTER

Glory, glory to the Father!
Glory, glory to the Son!
Glory, glory to the Spirit!
Glory to the Three in One!

MARGARET J. HARRIS

The task God's wisdom has assigned, let me
cheerfully fulfill.

CHARLES WESLEY

To Him I owe my life and breath, and all the
joys I have.

SAMUEL STENNETT

Praise the Lord: ye heavens adore Him;
Praise Him, angels in the height;
Sun and moon, rejoice before Him;
Praise Him, all ye stars of light.

EDWARD OSLER

Age to age God's power shall teach.

RICHARD MANT

How sure is joy for all who turn to You with an
undivided heart.

LAWRENCE TUTTIETT

Praise the Savior, all who know Him!

THOMAS KELLY

Happy day, happy day, when Jesus washed my
sins away.

PHILIP DODDRIDGE

Jesus comes in sounds of gladness, leading souls
   redeemed to heaven.

GODFREY THRING

Let all, with heart and voice,
Before His throne rejoice.

CHRISTIAN H. BATEMAN

Birds with gladder songs o'erflow,
Flowers with deeper beauties shine,
Since I know, as now I know,
I am His, and He is mine.

GEORGE W. ROBINSON

Ten thousand, thousand, precious gifts
My daily thanks employ;
Nor is the least a cheerful heart
That tastes those gifts with joy.

JOSEPH ADDISON

Father of mercies,
   in Your Word what endless glory shines!

ANNE STEELE

When resting in God's mighty hands, our hearts
   are filled with gladness.

N. F. S. GRUNDTVIG

In a world where Jesus reigns, there is gladness
    everywhere.

MARGARET E. SANGSTER

Fling wide the portals of your heart;
Make it a temple, set apart
Adorned with prayer, and love, and joy.

GEORG WEISSEL

Let the time of joy return.

WILLIAM HAMMOND

Bless, O my soul, the living God.

ISAAC WATTS

Stay Thou all my thoughts on Thee,
That the world may not annoy
While I make Thy Word my joy.

BENJAMIN SCHMOLCK

When your heart with joy o'erflowing,
Sings a thankful prayer,
In your joy, O let your brother
With you share.

THEODORE G. WILLIAMS

You have put gladness in my heart; then may I
    well be glad!

FRANCES R. HAVERGAL

The stormy sea sings praise to God, the thunder
  and the shower.

HENRY WARE, JR.

Bright youth and snow-crowned age,
Strong men and maidens fair,
Raise high your free, exulting song,
God's wondrous praise declare.

EDWARD H. PLUMPTRE

My thirst was quenched, my soul revived, and
  now I live in Him.

HORATIUS BONAR

From the cross the radiance streaming adds
  more luster to each day.

JOHN BOWRING

Happy the home where Jesus' Name
  is sweet to every ear.

HENRY WARE, JR.

I trace the rainbow through the rain,
And feel the promise is not vain
That morning shall tearless be.

GEORGE MATHESON

My God, I thank You, who has made
The earth so bright,
So full of splendor and of joy,
Beauty and light;
So many glorious things are here,
Noble and right.

ADELAIDE A. PROCTER

Hark! the voice of Jesus calling,
Who will go and work today?
Fields are white, the harvest waiting,
Who will bear the sheaves away?
Loud and long the Master calleth,
Rich reward He offers free;
Who will answer, gladly saying,
"Here am I, O Lord, send me."

DANIEL MARCH

My Master was a worker,
With daily work to do,
And he who would be like Him,
Must be a worker, too:
Then welcome honest labor,
And honest labor's fare,
For where there is a worker
The Master's man is there.

WILLIAM G. TARRANT

Were I a nightingale, I would act the part of a
    nightingale; were I a swan, the part of a
    swan. But I am a rational creature, and I
    ought to praise God.

EPICTETUS

Praise the Lord in every breath, let all things
    praise the Lord.

CHARLES WESLEY

May no earth-born cloud arise,
To hide You from Your servant's eyes.

JOHN KEBLE

O Savior, precious Savior mine!
What will Thy presence be,
If such a life of joy can crown
Our walk on earth with Thee?

FRANCES R. HAVERGAL

Saints below, with heart and voice,
Still in songs of praise rejoice,
Learning here, by faith and love,
Songs of praise to sing above.

JAMES MONTGOMERY

Let everlasting thanks be Thine
For such a bright display,
As makes a world of darkness shine
With beams of heavenly day.

WILLIAM COWPER

Think what Spirit dwells within me; what a
  Father's smile is mine.

HENRY F. LYTE

They who seek in God their rest, shall ever find
  Him near!

PAUL GERHARDT

Lift up your heart, lift up your voice!
Rejoice, again I say, rejoice!

CHARLES WESLEY

Come, Christians, join to sing
Loud praise to Christ our King;
Let all, with heart and voice,
Before His throne rejoice.

CHRISTIAN H. BATEMAN

Sing of Peace

Come unto Me, ye weary,
And I will give you rest.
O blessed voice of Jesus,
Which comes to hearts oppressed!
It tells of benediction,
Of pardon, grace and peace,
Of joy that has no ending,
Of love which cannot cease.

WILLIAM C. DIX

I come to cast myself on You: You are my rest.

CHARLOTTE ELLIOTT

In His arms He'll take and shield me.

JOSEPH SCRIVEN

I fear no foe, with You at hand to bless;
Ills have no weight, and tears no bitterness.

HENRY F. LYTE

As a mother stills her child,
You, Lord, can hush the ocean wild.

EDWARD HOPPER

Be still, my soul: the waves and winds still
    know
His voice who ruled them while He dwelt
    below.

KATHARINA VON SCHLEGEL

Like a river glorious, God's perfect peace, flows
  fuller every day, grows deeper all the way.
FRANCES R. HAVERGAL

I know this saving faith—believing in His Word
  brought peace within my heart.
DANIEL W. WHITTLE

Fear not; I am with you, O be not dismayed,
For I am your God, I will still give you aid.
"K" in RIPPON'S SELECTION of HYMNS

He leads me on through all the unquiet years;
Past all my dreamland hopes, and doubts, and
  fears.
HIRAM O. WILEY

Just as I am, though tossed about
With many a conflict, many a doubt,
Fightings and fears within, without,
O Lamb of God, I come!
CHARLOTTE ELLIOTT

Haste to your heavenly Father's throne, and
  sweet refreshment find.
PHILIP DODDRIDGE

He owns me for His child; I can no longer fear.
CHARLES WESLEY

To me, O Lord, Your grace impart,
Each trial to abide,
And let my heart
Find refuge at Your side.

M. LOY

Be my shield and hiding place.

JOHN NEWTON

What need I fear? What earthly grief or care,
since You are ever near, Jesus, my Lord.

JAMES G. DECK

Trust in His promises, faithful and sure.

WILLIAM A. OGDEN

That peace which flows serene and deep, a river
in the soul, whose banks a living verdure
keep, God's sunshine o'er the whole.

ANONYMOUS

Come, and in Jesus you will find a loving
Friend and kind.

JOHN M. WIGNER

The Lord is our Refuge, and whom can we
fear?

ANONYMOUS

The world's fierce winds are blowing
Temptations sharp and keen;
I feel a peace in knowing,
My Savior stands between.

ANONYMOUS

We bless Thee for Thy peace, God, deep as the
    unfathomed sea.

ANONYMOUS

There's not a plant or flower below, but makes
    Your glories known.

ISAAC WATTS

Speak through the earthquake, wind, and fire,
    O still small voice of calm!

JOHN GREENLEAF WHITTIER

Christ every grief has known
That wrings the human breast,
And takes and bears them for His own,
That all in Him may rest.

MATTHEW BRIDGES

Jesus! the Name that charms my fears, that bids
    my sorrows cease.

CHARLES WESLEY

Fountain of grace, rich, full and free,
What need I, that is not in Thee?
Full pardon, strength to meet the day,
And peace which none can take away.

JAMES EDMESTON

Let Thy Spirit now impart full salvation to my
    heart.

WILLIAM HAMMOND

Peace, perfect peace, with loved ones far away?
In Jesus' keeping we are safe, and they.

EDWARD H. BICKERSTETH

Things that once were wild alarms
Cannot now disturb my rest;
Closed in everlasting arms,
Pillowed on His loving breast.

GEORGE W. ROBINSON

Blest are the sons of peace whose hearts and
    hopes are one.

ISAAC WATTS

Take time to be holy, the world rushes on;
    spend much time in secret with Jesus alone.

WILLIAM D. LONGSTAFF

Blessed quietness, holy quietness, what
    assurance in my soul!

MARIE P. FERGUSON

That peace which suffers and is strong, trusts
    where it cannot see.

ANONYMOUS

O hidden source of calm repose,
All sufficient love divine,
My help and refuge from my foes,
Secure I am if You are mine.

CHARLES WESLEY

You are our joy and our rest.

PHILIP DODDRIDGE

O give Your own sweet rest to me,
That I may speak with soothing power;
To weary ones in needful hour.

FRANCES R. HAVERGAL

Your wants shall be His care.

NAHUM TATE and NICHOLAS BRADY

Bless the truth, dear Lord, to me,
As you blessed the bread by Galilee.
MARY A. LATHBURY

I love to steal away and spend the hours of
setting day in humble, grateful prayer.
PHOEBE H. BROWNE

Lead us, O Father, in the paths of peace.
WILLIAM H. BURLEIGH

So shall my walk be close with God, so purer
light shall mark the road that leads me to
the Lamb.
WILLIAM COWPER

Take from our souls the strain and stress,
And let our ordered lives confess
The beauty of Thy peace.
JOHN GREENLEAF WHITTIER

Calmly, dear Lord, on Thee we rest.
WILLIAM GASKELL

His Name shall be the Counsellor, the mighty
Prince of Peace.
WILLIAM H. CLARK

Keep me calm, calm in the closet's solitude,
  calm in the busy street.

HORATIUS BONAR

May our bounteous God, through all our life be
  near us.

MARTIN RINKART

Grant us Your peace throughout our life.

JOHN ELLERTON

Give me a calm, a thankful heart,
From every murmur free;
The blessings of Your grace impart,
And let me live for Thee.

ANNE STEELE

Lord, I would clasp Your hand in mine.

JOSEPH H. GILMORE

The Lord is my Shepherd; no want shall I know.
I feed in green pastures; safe-folded I rest.
He leadeth my soul where the still waters flow,
Restores me when wandering, redeems when
  oppressed.

JAMES MONTGOMERY

The storm may roar without me,
My heart may low be laid;
But God is round about me,
And can I be dismayed?

ANNE L. WARING

Calm me, my God, and keep me calm,
Soothe me with holy hymn and psalm,
And bid my spirit rest.

HORATIUS BONAR

For peaceful homes and healthful days,
For all the blessings earth displays,
We owe Thee thankfulness and praise
Who gives it all.

CHRISTOPHER WORDSWORTH

Sing
of
Patience

Wait, my soul, upon the Lord.

WILLIAM F. LLOYD

Your eternal love keeps on.

ISAAC WATTS

God leads us on by paths we do not know;
Upward He leads us, though our steps be slow;
Though oft we faint and falter on the way,
Though storms and darkness oft obscure the day,
Yet, when the clouds are gone,
We know He leads us on.

HIRAM O. WILEY

I've heard the Voice of my Savior, telling me still
to fight on; He promised never to leave me.

ANONYMOUS

Have we trials and temptations?
Is there trouble anywhere?
Jesus knows our every weakness,
Take it to the Lord in prayer.

JOSEPH SCRIVEN

May all my life, in every step, be fellowship
with Thee.

HORATIUS BONAR

Jesus comes in joy and sorrow,
Shares alike our hopes and fears;
Jesus comes, whate'er befalls us,
Glads our hearts, and dries our tears.

GODFREY THRING

Look down on me, for I am weak, and You are
my strength.

CHARLOTTE ELLIOTT

Wait but a little while
In uncomplaining love!
His own most gracious smile
Shall welcome you above.

HENRY W. BAKER

When all around my soul gives way, He then is
all my hope.

EDWARD MOTE

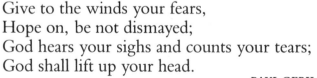

Give to the winds your fears,
Hope on, be not dismayed;
God hears your sighs and counts your tears;
God shall lift up your head.

PAUL GERHARDT

Ever faithful, ever faithful to the Truth may we
    be found.

JOHN FAWCETT

Yes, all my hope is in the Lord,
And not in my own merit;
I rest upon His faithful Word.
To them of contrite Spirit,
He's ever merciful and just.
Here is my comfort and my trust;
His help I wait with patience.

MARTIN LUTHER

Only be still, and wait His leisure
In cheerful hope, with heart content
To take whate'er Thy Father's pleasure
And all deserving love hath sent;
Nor doubt our inmost wants are known
To Him who chose us for His own.

GEORG NEUMARK

Let me only think of Thee,
And then new heart springs up in me.

SAMUEL LONGFELLOW

Through waves and clouds and storms, He
    gently clears my way.

PAUL GERHARDT

All our inmost wants are known
To Him who chose us for His own.

GEORG NEUMARK

Let us now be up and doing,
Nor our onward course abate;
Still achieving, still pursuing,
Learn to labor and to wait.

HENRY WADSWORTH LONGFELLOW

Lead us, O Father, to Thy heavenly rest,
However rough and steep the path may be,
Through joy or sorrow, as You deem it best,
Until our lives are perfected in Thee.

WILLIAM H. BURLEIGH

Jesus, my strength, my hope.

CHARLES WESLEY

Rest beside the weary road, and hear the angels
    sing.

EDMUND H. SEARS

A mighty fortress is our God, a bulwark never
    failing.

MARTIN LUTHER

Breathe on me, Breath of God, until my heart is
    pure.

EDWIN HATCH

Daily our lives would show
Some deed of kindness done,
Some soul by patience won,
Dear Lord, for Thee.

EDWIN P. PARKER

'Tis only in Christ
I feel my life secure;
In Him alone abiding,
All conflict can endure.

JAMES G. DECK

The murmuring wind, the quivering leaf shall
    softly tell us You are near!

OLIVER WENDELL HOLMES

Hope wipes the tear from sorrow's eye,
And faith points upward to the sky.

ANNE STEELE

A pilgrim and a stranger,
I journey here below,
Far distant is my country,
The home to which I go.

PAUL GERHARDT

Not enjoyment, and not sorrow,
Is our destined end or way;
But to act, that each tomorrow
Find us better than today.

HENRY WADSWORTH LONGFELLOW

The work of faith will not be done till I obtain
    my crown.

GEORGE HEATH

In keenest strife, Lord, may we stand,
Upheld and strengthened by Thy hand.

GEORGE T. COSTER

We shall come rejoicing, bringing in the sheaves.

KNOWLES SHAW

My soul rejoices to pursue the steps of Him
    I love.

WILLIAM COWPER

Nor shall Thy spreading gospel rest
Till Christ has all the nations blessed.

ISAAC WATTS

Sing
of
Goodness

I sing the goodness of the Lord, that filled the
    earth with food; He formed the creatures
    with His Word, and then pronounced them
    good.

ISAAC WATTS

Through You the deserts laugh and sing,
And nature smiles and owns her King.

HENRY F. LYTE

God's goodness stands approved, unchanged
    from day to day.

PHILIP DODDRIDGE

O God, thou giver of all good,
Thy children live by daily food;
And daily must the prayer be said,
"Give us this day our daily bread."

SAMUEL LONGFELLOW

Good Shepherd, may I sing Thy praise within
    Thy house forever.

HENRY W. BAKER

He knows and He approves the way the
    righteous go.

ISAAC WATTS

The year is with Your goodness crowned.

HENRY F. LYTE

The hills leap up in gladness, the valleys laugh
    and sing.

JOHN S. B. MONSELL

How wondrous and great Thy work, God
    of praise!

HENRY USTIC ONDERDONK

All through the length of our days, Your
    goodness never fails.

HENRY W. BAKER

My God, You do all things well.

M. LOY

Jesus paid it all, all to Him I owe.

ELVINA M. HALL

Lord Jesus, I long to be perfectly whole;
I want You forever to live in my soul.

JAMES NICHOLSON

He, only, could unlock the gate of heaven and
    let us in.

CECIL F. ALEXANDER

To them that seek Thee, Thou art good; to
    them that find Thee, Thou art all.

BERNARD of CLAIRVAUX

Blessed be the Name of Jesus!

MARGARET J. HARRIS

Help us, dear Lord, this and every day,
To live more nearly as we pray.

JOHN KEBLE

Run the straight race through God's good grace,
Lift up your eyes, and seek His face.

JOHN S. B. MONSELL

Let our lips and lives express the holy gospel
    we profess.

ISAAC WATTS

Christ died that we might be forgiven. He died
    to make us good.

CECIL F. ALEXANDER

Your Word is like the sun, a heavenly light,
That guides us all the day;
And through the dangers of the night,
A lamp to lead our way.

ISAAC WATTS

I praise Thee for the desert road, and for the
    riverside.

JANE CREWDSON

Let Thy grace, Lord, like a fetter, bind my
    wandering heart to Thee.

ROBERT ROBINSON

May our hands be pure from stain
With which our daily bread we gain.

SAMUEL LONGFELLOW

Blest are the pure in heart, for they shall see
    our God.

JOHN KEBLE

By day, by night, at home, abroad,
Still are we guarded by our God;
By His incessant bounty fed,
By His unerring counsel led.

PHILIP DODDRIDGE

Sing
of
Kindness

We thank Thee, Lord, for our food, for life and
    health and every good.

JOHN CENNICK

How gentle God's commands! How kind His
    precepts are!

PHILIP DODDRIDGE

All the plenty summer pours;
Autumn's rich o'erflowing stores;
Flocks that whiten all the plain;
Yellow sheaves of ripened grain:
Lord, for these our souls shall raise
Grateful vows and solemn praise.

ANNA L. BARBAULD

Thy hand sets fast the mighty hills,
Thy voice the troubled ocean stills;
Evening and morning hymn Thy praise,
And earth Thy bounty wide displays.

HENRY F. LYTE

O give us hearts to love like You!

JOHN S. B. MONSELL

He whose love has wisely schooled me,
And whose hand has gently ruled me,
Will not leave me now to pine.

ANONYMOUS

The Lord is never far away.

JOHANN J. SCHUTZ

The lambs in His bosom He tenderly bears, and
brings back the wanderers all safe from
the snares.

ANONYMOUS

Deep and precious, strong and gracious is the
Word of God above.

T. V. OLDENBURG

Sweet is the tender love Jesus has shown.

WILLIAM A. OGDEN

Children of the heavenly King,
As you journey, sweetly sing;
Sing your Savior's worthy praise,
Glorious in His works and ways.

JOHN CENNICK

In His hands He gently bears us, rescues us
from all our foes.

HENRY F. LYTE

As Thy prospering hand hath blest,
May we give Thee of our best.

ANNA L. BARBAULD

Then bless His holy Name,
Whose grace has made me whole,
Whose loving-kindness crowns my days!
O bless the Lord, my soul!

JAMES MONTGOMERY

Come, cast your burdens on the Lord,
and trust His constant care.

PHILIP DODDRIDGE

A whispered word may touch the heart, and call
it back to life.

ANONYMOUS

Spirit of grace, be ever nigh.

ANNE STEELE

My Master was a helper,
The woes of life He knew,
And he who would be like Him,
Must be a helper, too.

WILLIAM G. TARRANT

For the grandeur of God's nature,
Grand beyond a seraph's thought;
For the wonders of creation,
Works with skill and kindness wrought;
For His providence that governs
Through His empire's wide domain,
Wings an angel, guides a sparrow,
Blessed be His gentle reign.

ROBERT ROBINSON

Perverse and foolish oft I strayed,
But yet in love He sought me,
And on His shoulder gently laid
And home, rejoicing brought me.

HENRY W. BAKER

Far as east from west is distant,
He hath put away our sin;
Like the pity of a father
Hath the Lord's compassion been.

UNITED PRESBYTERIAN BOOK OF PSALMS, 1871

O fill me with Thy fulness, Lord, until my
　　heart overflows.

FRANCES R. HAVERGAL

Even in the darkest spot of earth, God's love
　　is found.

ADELAIDE A. PROCTER

To the Holy Spirit,
Who does upon us pour
His blessed dews and sunshine,
Be praise for evermore.

JOHN S. B. MONSELL

Sing to the great Jehovah's praise!
All praise to Him belongs;
Who kindly lengthens out our days,
Inspires our choicest songs.

CHARLES WESLEY

The Lord to me is kind.

JAMES MONTGOMERY

Sing
of
Meekness

Through cloud and sunshine, abide with me.

HENRY F. LYTE

Be with me, Lord, where'er I go: teach me
what You would have me do.

JOHN CENNICK

In me, through me, with me ever, Lord
accomplish Your will.

*LUDAEMILIA ELIZABETH of
SCHWARZBURG-RUDOLSTADT*

Still to the lowly soul
God does Himself impart,
And selects the pure in heart.

JOHN KEBLE

O use me, Lord, use even me, until Your
blessed face I see.

FRANCES R. HAVERGAL

Spirit of God, descend upon my heart; and
make me love Thee as I ought to love.

GEORGE CROLY

Fill our hearts with Thy rich grace.

WILLIAM HAMMOND

O wondrous Lord, my soul would be
Still more and more conformed to Thee.
A. CLEVELAND COXE

Prevent me, lest I harbor pride,
Lest I in my own strength confide;
Show me my weakness, let me see
I have my power, my all from Thee.
JOHN CENNICK

Take my life, and let it be
Consecrated, Lord, to Thee;
Take my hands, and let them move
At the impulse of Thy love.

Take my feet, and let them be
Swift and beautiful for Thee;
Take my voice, and let me sing
Always, only, for my King.
FRANCES R. HAVERGAL

Lead me, Father, in the paths of truth.
WILLIAM H. BURLEIGH

Stand up, stand up for Jesus,
Stand in His strength alone.
GEORGE DUFFIELD

Two wonders I confess:
The wonder of His glorious love
And my unworthiness.

ELIZABETH C. CLEPHANE

Jesus! Name of wondrous love!
Unto Thee must every knee
Bow in deep humility.

WILLIAM W. HOW

What You shall today provide, let me as a
    child receive.

JOHN NEWTON

Holy Spirit, all divine, dwell within this heart
    of mine.

ANDREW REED

O happy home, where each one serves Christ,
    whatever his appointed work may be.

CARL J. P. SPITTA

Help me to put my house in order,
That I may ever ready be
To leave this world and say in meekness:
Lord, as You will, deal with me.

EMILIE JULIANE

O come, and dwell in me, spirit of power within.

CHARLES WESLEY

Where meek souls will receive Him still, the dear
Christ enters in.

PHILLIPS BROOKS

Break Thou the bread of life,
Dear Lord, to me,
As Thou didst break the loaves
Beside the sea.

MARY A. LATHBURY

As Your angels serve before You, so on earth
Your will be done.

EDWARD OSLER

Make friends of God's children;
Help those who are weak,
Forgetting in nothing
His blessing to seek.

WILLIAM D. LONGSTAFF

The nations all whom You have made
Shall come, and all shall frame
To bow them low before You, Lord,
And glorify Your Name.

JOHN MILTON

God is with all that serve the right, the holy,
    true, and free.

ANONYMOUS

My gracious Master and my God,
Assist me to proclaim,
To spread through all the earth abroad,
The honors of Thy Name.

CHARLES WESLEY

At the Name of Jesus every knee shall bow,
Every tongue confess Him King of Glory now.

CAROLINE M. NOEL

In God, our shield, we will rejoice, and ever
bless Your Name.

NAHUM TATE and NICHOLAS BRADY

Sing
of
Faith

Oh, what peace we often forfeit,
Oh, what needless pain we bear,
All because we do not carry
Everything to God in prayer!

JOSEPH SCRIVEN

Why restless, why cast down, my soul?
Hope still, and you shall sing
The praise of Him who is your God,
Your Savior, and your King.

NAHUM TATE and NICHOLAS BRADY

Wherever He shall guide me,
No want shall turn me back;
My Shepherd is beside me,
And nothing can I lack.

ANNE L. WARING

His Name above all names shall stand, exalted
more and more.

WILLIAM H. CLARK

That hand which bears all nature up shall guard
His children well.

PHILIP DODDRIDGE

The unwearied sun from day to day,
Does the Creator's power display;
And publishes to every land,
The work of an Almighty Hand.

JOSEPH ADDISON

O for a faith that will not shrink!

WILLIAM H. BATHURST

Who upholds and comforts us in all trials, fears,
and needs. Blest and Holy Trinity, praise
forever be to You!

TOBIAS CLAUSNITZER

I have no help but Thine, nor do I need another
arm save Thine to lean upon.

HORATIUS BONAR

Grant us light that we may know the wisdom
You alone can give.

LAWRENCE TUTTIETT

Lead, kindly Light amid the encircling gloom,
lead Thou me on; the night is dark, and I
am far from home; lead Thou me on.

JOHN H. NEWMAN

There's no one to save us but Jesus;
   there's no other way but His way.
                                    GEORGE F. ROOT

O blessed life! the soul that soars,
Beyond the sense—beyond to Him
Whose love unlocks the heavenly doors.
                                    WILLIAM T. MATSON

Your Word is everlasting truth,
How pure is every page;
That holy book shall guide our youth,
And well support our age.

                                    ISAAC WATTS

What I read, help me to heed it; what You say,
   O let me do.
                                    BENJAMIN SCHMOLCK

Our God preserves the souls of those who on
   His truth depend.
                                    NAHUM TATE and NICHOLAS BRADY

O let us all with one accord
Sing praises to our heavenly Lord.
                                    ENGLISH CAROL

Well God knows what best to grant me; when
   He speaks, I will obey.
                                    ANONYMOUS

Sweet is the confidence of faith.

AUGUSTUS M. TOPLADY

O Christ, by whom we come to God, Lord,
    teach us how to pray.

JAMES MONTGOMERY

What a privilege to carry everything to God
    in prayer!

JOSEPH SCRIVEN

When we disclose our wants in prayer, may we
    our wills resign to You.

JOSEPH D. CARLYLE

I wholly lean on Jesus' Name.

EDWARD MOTE

My Jesus, as Thou wilt! My Lord Thy will
    be done.

BENJAMIN SCHMOLCK

Father, Thy Name be praised, Thy kingdom
    given, Thy will be done on earth as it is in
    heaven; keep us in life, forgive our sins,
    deliver us now and ever.

BOHEMIAN BRETHREN

God never yet forsook a need of a soul that
trusted Him.

GEORG NEUMARK

Wide as the world is His command;
Vast as eternity His love;
Firm as a rock His truth will stand.

ISAAC WATTS

I, the Lord, am with thee,
Be not then afraid;
I will help and strengthen,
Be then not dismayed.

Yea, I will uphold thee
With Mine Own right hand;
Thou art called and chosen
In My sight to stand.

Onward then, and fear not,
Children of the day;
For His Word shall never,
Never pass away.

FRANCES R. HAVERGAL

I see You not, I hear You not; yet You are often
with me.

RAY PALMER

From everlasting Thou art God, to endless years
the same.

ISAAC WATTS

God moves in a mysterious way
His wonders to perform;
He plants His footsteps in the sea,
And rides upon the storm.

WILLIAM COWPER

Only Thou art holy; there is none beside Thee
Perfect in power, in love, in purity.

ISAAC WATTS

You, O Lord, and You alone, are God from
all eternity.

NAHUM TATE and NICHOLAS BRADY

Our God preserves the souls of those
Who on His truth depend;
To them and their posterity
His blessing shall descend.

NAHUM TATE and NICHOLAS BRADY

Never shall His promise fail.

EDWARD OSLER

The Church's one foundation is Jesus Christ
her Lord.

SAMUEL J. STONE

On Christ, the solid Rock, I stand.

EDWARD MOTE

Praise the God of our salvation.

EDWARD OSLER

Christ, whose glory fills the skies,
Christ, the true, the only Light,
Dayspring from on high, be near;
Daystar, in my heart appear.

CHARLES WESLEY

God is my strong salvation: what have I to fear
   with God at my right hand?

JAMES MONTGOMERY

Pilot me over life's tempestuous sea.

EDWARD HOPPER

Jesus comes! He fills my soul!
Perfected in Him I am;
I am complete, made whole;
Glory, glory to the Lamb!

WILLIAM McDONALD

Yes, Jesus is the truth, the way, that leads us
   into rest.

JOHN H. STOCKTON

Trust His Word.

GEORG NEUMARK

Trust His love for all to come.

ANONYMOUS

I, the Lord, am with thee,
Be not afraid;
I will help and strengthen thee,
Be not dismayed.

FRANCES R. HAVERGAL

Yet though I have not seen, and still
Must rest in faith alone,
I love Thee, dearest Lord,—and will,
Unseen, but not unknown.

RAY PALMER

He who feeds the ravens, will give His
       children bread.

WILLIAM COWPER

Only believe, and you shall see
That Christ is all to thee.

JOHN S. B. MONSELL

What yet we shall be none can tell:
Now we are His, and all is well.

LUCY LARCOM

Sing of Heaven

If on a quiet sea,
Toward heaven we calmly sail,
With grateful hearts O God, to Thee,
We'll own the favoring gale.

AUGUSTUS M. TOPLADY

The day must dawn, and dark night be past;
And heaven, the heart's true home, will come
at last.

FREDERICK W. FABER

O let us in His Name sing on,
And hasten to that day
When our Redeemer shall come down,
And shadows pass away.

CHARLES WESLEY

Lift your eyes, you sons of light,
Zion's city is in sight;
There our endless home shall be,
There our Lord we soon shall see.

JOHN CENNICK

Be still, my soul; when change and tears are past,
All safe and blessed we shall meet at last.

KATHARINA VON SCHLEGEL

Christ is the way, the truth, the life; grant us
    that way to know.

                   GEORGE W. DOANE

Awake, my soul.

                   MATTHEW BRIDGES

King of kings in heaven we'll crown Him, when
    our journey is complete.

                 LYDIA BAXTER

Scatter all my unbelief;
More and more Yourself display,
Shining to the perfect day.

                 CHARLES WESLEY

Not for myself alone may my prayers be.
Lift Thou Thy world, O Christ, closer to Thee.

                 LUCY LARCOM

Fight the good fight with all thy might;
Christ is thy strength, and Christ thy light.
Lay hold on life, and it shall be
Thy joy and crown eternally.

             JOHN S. B. MONSELL

Though clouds may surround us, our God is
    our light;
Though storms rage around us, our God is
    our might.

             ANONYMOUS

Rejoice, in glorious hope!
Our Lord the Judge shall come,
And take His servants up
To their eternal home.　　　　*CHARLES WESLEY*

Jesus comes again in glory,
Let us then our homage pay,
Alleluia! Alleluia!　　　　*GODFREY THRING*

Through every period of my life Your goodness
　　I'll proclaim; and after death, in distant
　　worlds, resume the glorious theme.
　　　　　　　　　　JOSEPH ADDISON

Let me among Your saints be found, when the
　　archangel's trumpet sounds, to see Your
　　smiling face.
　　　　　　　　　　LADY HUNTINGDON

Hallelujah! what a Savior!
　　　　　　　　　　PHILIP P. BLISS

Praise Him, ye saints, the God of love
Who hath my sins forgiven,
Till, gathered to the Church above,
We sing the songs of heaven.
　　　　　　　　　　CHARLES WESLEY

Eternity's too short to utter all Your praise.
　　　　　　　　　　JOSEPH ADDISON

Jesus! the very thought of Thee
With sweetness fills my breast:
But sweeter far Thy face to see,
And in Thy presence rest.

att. to BERNARD of CLAIRVAUX

Teach me to live, dear Lord, only for Thee
As Thy disciples lived in Galilee.

MARY A. LATHBURY

Give us the wisdom so to spend each passing
    moment that we at length may live
       with Thee.

HARRIET AUBER

Thou will my every want supply.

CHARLOTTE ELLIOTT

When the toil is over, then come rest and peace.

THOMAS J. POTTER

Accept these hands that labor,
My heart to trust and love,
And be with me and hasten
Your kingdom from above.

JOHN S. B. MONSELL

To him that in Thy Name believes, eternal life
    with Thee is given.

CHARLES WESLEY

Guard us waking, guard us sleeping,
And when we die,
May we be in Your keeping.

REGINALD HEBER

His reign no end shall know.

JOHN MORRISON

Thy beauty, Lord, and glory,
The wonders of Thy love,
Shall be the endless story
Of all Thy saints above.

JAMES G. DECK

Lord Jesus, think on me.

SYNESIUS of CYRENE

Jesus, Thou Prince of Life,
Thy chosen cannot die;
Like Thee, they conquer in the strife,
To reign with Thee on high.

H. A. CAESAR MALAN

We are watching, we are waiting, for the Light,
the Truth, the Way.

ANONYMOUS

Light of Light, shine o'er us on our pilgrim way.

WILLIAM W. HOW

Book design by John DiLorenzo
Cover and interior art by Peter Church
Typeset in BEMBO